THE WORK
OF A
COMMON WOMAN

Also by Judy Grahn:

Edward the Dyke and Other Poems
The Common Woman Poems
A Woman Is Talking to Death
She Who
Where Would I Be Without You: The Poetry of
    Judy Grahn and Pat Parker (Olyvia Records)
True to Life Adventure Stories, Vol's I and II (ed.)
The Queen of Wands
Another Mother Tongue
The Queen of Swords
Mundane's World, A Novel

THE WORK OF A COMMON WOMAN

THE COLLECTED POETRY OF
JUDY GRAHN
1964 - 1977

WITH AN INTRODUCTION BY
ADRIENNE RICH

THE CROSSING PRESS
Freedom, CA 95019

Copyright © 1978 by Judy Grahn
Originally published by Diana Press, reissued by St. Martin's Press

Cover design by Diana Souza
Book design by Wendy Cadden
Graphics on pages 59, 62, 64, 66, 70, 72, 75, and 133 by
    Wendy Cadden
Graphics on pages 23 and 111 by Karen Sjoholm

Library of Congress Cataloging in Publication Data

Grahn, Judy.
    The work of a common woman.

    I. Title.
PS3557.R226W6 1980 1980 813'.54 79-27318
ISBN 0-89594-156-2
ISBN 0-89594-155-4 (pbk.)

CONTENTS

POWER AND DANGER:
THE WORK OF A COMMON WOMAN by JUDY GRAHN

The necessity of poetry has to be stated over and over, but only to those who have reason to fear its power, or those who still believe that language is "only words" and that an old language is good enough for our descriptions of the world we are trying to transform.

For many women, the commonest words are having to be sifted through, rejected, laid aside for a long time, or turned to the light for new colors and flashes of meaning: *power, love, control, violence, political, personal, private, friendship, community, sexual, work, pain, pleasure, self, integrity* ... When we become acutely, disturbingly aware of the language we are using and that is using us, we begin to grasp a material resource that women have never before collectively attempted to repossess (though we were its inventors, and though individual writers like Dickinson, Woolf, Stein, H. D., have approached language as transforming power.) Language is as real, as tangible in our lives as streets, pipelines, telephone switchboards, microwaves, radioactivity, cloning laboratories, nuclear power stations. We might, hypothetically, possess ourselves of every recognized technological resource on the North American continent, but as long as our language is inadequate, our vision remains formless, our thinking and feeling are still running in the old cycles, our process may be "revolutionary" but not transformative.

For many of us, the word "revolution" itself has become not only a dead relic of Leftism, but a key to the dead-endedness of male politics: the "revolution" of a wheel which returns in the end to the same place; the "revolving door" of a politics which has "liberated" women only to use them, and only within the limits of male tolerance. When we speak of *transformation* we speak more accurately out of the vision of a process which will leave neither surfaces nor depths unchanged, which enters society at the most essential level of the subjugation of women and nature by men. We begin to conceive a planet on which both women and nature might coexist as the She Who we encounter in Judy Grahn's poems.

Poetry is, among other things, a criticism of language. In setting words together in new configurations, in the mere, immense shift from male to female pronouns, in the relationships between words created through echo, repetition, rhythm, rhyme, it lets us hear and see our words in a new dimension:

> *I am the wall at the lip of the water*
> *I am the rock that refused to be battered*
> *I am the dyke in the matter, the other*
> *I am the wall with the womanly swagger...*

Poetry is above all a concentration of the *power* of language, which is the power of our ultimate relationship to everything in the universe. It is as if forces we can lay claim to in no other way, become present to us in sensuous form. The knowledge and use of this magic goes back very far: the rune; the chant; the incantation; the spell; the kenning; sacred words; forbidden words; the naming of the child, the plant, the insect, the ocean, the configuration of stars, the snow, the sensation in the body. The ritual telling of the dream. The physical reality of the human voice; of words gouged or incised in stone or wood, woven in silk or wool, painted on vellum, or traced in sand.

Forces we can lay claim to in no other way...Think of the deprivation of women living for centuries without a poetry which spoke of women together, of women alone, of women as anything but the fantasies of men. Think of the hunger unnamed and unnameable, the sensations mistranslated.

In January 1974, struggling with flu and a rising temperature, I lay in bed and turned the pages of a magazine to a poem called "A Woman Is Talking to Death". Its first three or four lines possessed an uncanny urgency, rare even among the strong poems that *Amazon Quarterly*—the magazine I held in my hands—had been publishing.* When I finished the poem I realized I had been weeping; and I knew in an exhausted kind of way that what had happened to me was irreversible. All I could do with it at that point was lie down and sleep, let the flu run its course, and the knowledge that was accumulating in my life, the poem I had just read, go on circulating in my bloodstream.

A week or two later I heard that Judy Grahn was giving a reading in New York, I went. A woman, who looked both slight and strong, got up in the darkish clutter of the Westbeth Artists' Project and started speaking in a low voice, first about the Oakland Women's Press Collective, which she had helped to found, then briefly about her own work. She read some poems from a pamphlet-sized book called "The Common Woman" and then, "A Woman Is Talking to Death". She read very quietly. I have never heard a poem

*I want here to pay tribute to that journal, which provided, in its brief life, a space in which thinking as a woman, loving women, and creating for women became fused, made more possible, in essay after essay, poem after poem, vision after vision.

encompassing so much violence, grief, anger, compassion, read so quietly. There was absolutely no false performance.

That evening she also read "A Plain Song from an Older Woman to a Younger Woman"—utterly different from, yet as extraordinary in its way as "A Woman Is Talking to Death": a poem of tender, bitter, lamentation, its rhymes and rhythms strung in a very old form, but its direction a new one for poetry: the "new words" which are written by women writing entirely to and for women. (The point, by the way, in case it need be made here in this book which so many will hold in their hands, is not the "exclusion" of men; it is that *primary presence of women to ourselves and each other* first described in prose by Mary Daly, and which is the crucible of a new language.)

Much later, some of us went out to get something to eat; and I was able to speak to Judy Grahn, rather haltingly, of the effect of her work on me. We were strangers, she even shyer than I, perhaps instinctively shy of New York. I remember her saying that writing "A Woman Is Talking to Death" had frightened her enough that she'd decided to stop writing poetry for awhile and work on a novel. But of course she didn't stop writing poetry. She continues work on the novel; but this collection shows that she has chosen to acknowledge the importance of her poetry as a body of work and as a path into the future.

I felt I could understand why she said writing the long poem had frightened her; it wasn't simply the routine hype of the travelling poet who is expected to give back provocative responses to compliments. I think any poet lives in both terror and longing for the poem which will bring together—

at least for the time being—everywhere she has been, everything her work to date has been a preparation for. "A Woman Is Talking to Death" feels like such a poem. Flashes of the poet's experience (*testimony in trials that never got heard*) intersect with images of death at work: historical violence against women, ranging from the feudal wife through the witches to the aging or teen-aged rape victim; the reduction of Black people, poor people, and women to non-human status; the violence—of neglect, of rejection, of outright brutality or accidental cruelty—that the powerless inflict on ourselves and each other; the sapping-away of female spirit and flesh by the culture of patriarchy. There is nothing more unnerving and yet empowering than the making of connections, and "A Woman Is Talking to Death" makes connections first for the poet, among events in her own life; then for us who live intensely, through the power of her language, what she has lived and seen. It is in the language of the poem that the fragments come together, echoing off each other in repetitions, in rhythms, in an intricate structure which may not be obvious on a first reading or hearing, but which works like the complexity of a piece of music. Nothing less complex could do justice to the "contradictions" of the games we play with death in a culture which not only blames the victim but sets the victim to blaming other victims, keeps the wheel of powerlessness spinning, dead motorcyclist to Black motorist to white woman outside the law fleeing the bridge in fear, the repetitions of history:

> keep the women small and weak
> and off the street, and off the
> bridges, that's the way, brother,
> one day I will leave you there,

as I have left you there before,
working for death.

Under the pressure of these contradictions, which are transformed into connections, words are forced to yield up new meanings in the poem: *lovers; I wanted her; indecent acts.* The word *lover,* purged of romantic-sentimental associations, becomes a name for what human beings might mean to each other in a world where each person held both power and responsibility. There are poems, which, as we write them, we know are going to change the ways in which it is possible for us to see and act. Perhaps "A Woman Is Talking to Death" was this kind of poem for Judy Grahn.

It has been this kind of poem for me, and I think for a great many of its readers. And I think it is a pivotal poem in this book.

"A Woman Is Talking to Death" is both a political poem and a love poem. I mean, that it is a political poem to the extent that it is a love poem, and a love poem insofar as it is political—that is, concerned with powerlessness and power. No true political poetry can be written with propaganda as an aim, to persuade others "out there" of some atrocity or injustice (hence the failure, as poetry, of so much anti-war poetry of the sixties). *As poetry,* it can come only from the poet's need to identify her relationship to atrocities and injustice, the sources of her pain, fear, and anger, the meaning of her resistance. Nor are we likely to write good love poems because, having "fallen in love" we want to lay a poem in the lover's lap. The gift-poem is usually unmeaningful to anyone but the recipient. The most revealing and life-sustaining love poetry is not "about" the lover but about the poet's attempt to live with her experience of love, to fathom how she can order its chaos and ride out its storms, to ask what *loving* an individual can mean in the face of death, cruelty, famine, violence, taboo. For the lesbian poet it means rejecting the entire convention of love-poetry and undertaking to create a new tradition. She is forced by the conditions under which she loves, and the conditions in which all women attempt to survive, to ask questions that never occurred to a Donne or a Yeats, or even to an Elizabeth Barrett Browning (whose love poems are conventional, though her political poems are not); questions about taboo, integrity, the fetishization of the female body, the world-wide historical violence committed against women by men, what it means to be "true to one another" when we are women, what it means to love women when that love is de-nied reality, treated as perversion, or, even more insidiously, "accepted" as a mirror-image or parallel to heterosexual romance. Judy Grahn, more than any other poet today, has taken up that challenge.

The book begins, interestingly, with a very early warning against the romantic convention. "Edward the Dyke" is a satire on the psychoanalysts and their "scientific" diagnosis and cures for lesbianism; but it is also a satire on lesbian romanticism. Edward indeed has a "problem", but it is not her "homosexuality"; rather it's that she has only a senti-mental and rhetorical language in which to describe her ex-perience: "Love flowers pearl, of delighted arms. Warm and water. Melting of vanilla wafer in the pants. Pink petal roses trembling overdew on the lips, soft and juicy fruit....Cinna-mon toast poetry. Justice equality higher wages. Independ-ent angel song. It means I can do what I want." The reverse of all this is her capitulation before the psychoanalyst's bul-lying: "I am vile! I am vile!" Because Edward has no sense of her love for women as anything but utopian, individual

and personal, she has no resistance to "treatment", in fact
seeks it out; she is easily turned against herself. The warning
of "Edward the Dyke" (and it is a serious one, couched in
an apparently witty and lighthearted fable) is that if you un-
questioningly accept one piece of the culture that despises
and fears you, you are vulnerable to other pieces. Language
is the key. Dr. Knox doesn't listen to anything Edward is
saying; but Edward herself fails to examine both the breath-
less language of her love *and* the language of the analyst's
version: "sordid...depraved...clandestine...penis envy...nar-
cissism...mother substitute". Only as we begin to ask our-
selves whether terms like "penis envy", "masochism", even
"homosexual" have any meaning, or what they are actually
describing, do we begin to create a language and worldview
of our own, to perceive the vast landscape of woman-hating
and male envy of women, underlying the haze of heterosex-
ual romance, the domestic idyll, and the jargon of "pathol-
ogy" and "deviance".

Over and over Grahn calls up the living woman against
the manufactured one, the man-made creation of centuries
of male art and literature. *Look at me as if you had never
seen a woman before...Our lovers teeth are white geese fly-
ing above us/ Our lovers muscles are rope-ladders under our
hands.* Marilyn Monroe's body, in death, becomes a weapon
her bone a bludgeon to beat the voyeurs, the fetishists, the
poets and journalists vampirizing off the "dumb-blonde" of
the centerfolds. *There were two long-haired women/ hold-
ing back the traffic just behind me/ with their bare hands,
the machines came down like mad bulls...*Loving women
means loving not a fantasy but women as we are, a woman
as she is:

> *wanting, wanting*
> *am I not   broken*
> *stolen   common*

am I not crinkled cranky poison
am I not glinty-eyed and frozen

am I not   aged

am I not   aged
shaky   glazing
am I not   hazy
guarded   craven

.   .   .

was I not   over
over   ridden?   (She Who)

She keeps her mind the way men
keep a knife—keen to strip the game
down to her size. She has a thin spine,
swallows her eggs cold, and tells lies...

(The Common Woman)

And it means above all asking questions about power:

if Love means protect then whenever I do not
defend you
I cannot call my name Love.
if Love means rebirth then when I see us
dead on our feet
I cannot call my name Love.
if Love means provide & I cannot
provide for you
why would you call my name Love?

(Confrontations...)

Powerless, women have been seduced into confusing love
with false power—the "power" of mother-love, the "power"
of gentle influence, the "power" of non-violence, the

"power" of the meek who are to inherit the earth. Grahn
conjures up other meanings of power:

> ...*Many years back*
> *a woman of strong purpose*
> *passed through this section*
> *and everything else tried to follow.*   *(She Who)*

> *was I not   ruling*
> *guiding   naming*
> *was I not   brazen*
> *crazy   chosen*
>
> *even the stones would do my bidding?*   *(She Who)*

> *Carol and her*
> *crescent wrench*
> *work bench*
> *wooden fence*
> *wide stance...*
> *Carol and her*
> *hack saw*
> *well worn*
> *torn back*
> *bad spine*
> *never-mind*
> *timberline*
> *clear mind...*   *(She Who)*

The power and danger of the lesbian converge in "A Woman

Is Talking to Death". *This woman is a lesbian, be careful.*
When after leaving the bridge where the motorcyclist was
killed, the narrator looks in the mirror, she sees:

> *...nobody was there to testify;*
> *how clear, an unemployed queer woman*
> *makes no witness at all,*
> *nobody at all was there for*
> *those two questions: what does*
> *she do, and who is she married to?*

Power and powerlessness: the original "Common Woman"
sequence is a study in this theme, besides being the most
vivid and clearhoned series of portraits of women in any
poetry I know. Each of these women is fighting in her own
way to gain a little control over her life: Helen trying to
grasp it at the price of "spite and malice", a "metallic" re-
spectability, a life in which "details take the place of mean-
ing"; Ella who "turns away the smaller tips, out of pride"
and who "shot a lover who misused her child" thereby los-
ing the child; Nadine who "holds things together, collects
bail...pokes at the ruins of the city/like an armored tank...";
Carol, forced to hide her strength on the job, who "walks
around all day/quietly, but underneath it/she's electric: an-
gry energy inside a passive form". Annie who "when she
smells danger...spills herself all over/like gasoline, and lights
it"; Margaret, "fired for making/strikes, and talking out of
turn/...Lusting for changes, she laughs through her/teeth,
and wanders from room to room"; Vera with her "religion
which insisted that people/are beautiful golden birds and
must be preserved".

The "Common Woman" is far more than a class descrip-
tion· What is "common" in and to women is the intersection

of oppression and strength, damage and beauty. It is, quite simply, the *ordinary* in women which will "rise" in every sense of the word—spiritually and in activism. For us, to be "extraordinary" or "uncommon" is to fail. History has been embellished with "extraordinary", "exemplary", "uncommon", and of course "token" women whose lives have left the rest unchanged. The "common woman" is in fact the embodiment of the extraordinary will-to-survive in millions of women, a life-force which transcends childbearing: unquenchable, chromosomatic reality. Only when we can count on this force in each other, everywhere, know absolutely that it is there for us, will we cease abandoning and being abandoned by "all of our lovers". Judy Grahn reclaims "the common woman" as a phrase from simplistic Marxist associations, or such political cliches as "the century of the common man."*

I think this passion for survival is the great theme of women's poetry (how interesting that male critics have focussed on our suicidal poets, and on their "self"- destructiveness rather than their capacity for hard work and for staying alive as long as they did. How expectable, yet how nauseating, the vogue for Julie Harris' sugared impersonation of Emily Dickinson as "The Belle of Amherst", depicting as a

---

*She also reclaims the lesbian from the visual stereotypes of male Decadent painters such as Egon Schiele, Aubrey Beardsley, Gustav Klimt, who represented lesbians as exotic hothouse flowers, elegantly and evilly erotic, and essentially predatory. Also, from the histroical impression derived from actual women such as Natalie Barney, Djuna Barnes, Renée Vivien, Radclyff Hall: an atmosphere of upperclass privilege, continental salons, high fashion, and trips to Lesbos. Or from the defiantly "exceptional" mode of Gertrude Stein (who would have indignantly rejected the term "common woman" as applied to herself, but who also suffered acutely from her sense of herself as a loner.)

neurasthenic "feminine" little eccentric the poet whose major themes were power and anger.) The poetry of female survival has its own history, but in it must be mentioned Juana de la Cruz, Louise Labé, the women troubadors, Emily Dickinson, Elizabeth Barrett Browning, Emily Brontë, H.D.—"Every woman who writes is a survivor", Tillie Olsen has said. Literacy, the time and space to make literature, were stolen from women by the patriarchal order. And when we could make literature, it has been lost, misread, kept from us. In my college years we studied the "great" long poems of modernism, Eliot's "The Waste Land", Hart Crane's "The Bridge", Pound's "Cantos", and later William Carlos William's "Paterson", Allen Ginsberg's "Howl". But we did not read, and courses in modern poetry still do not teach, H.D.'s epic poem, "Trilogy", in which she confronted war, nationalist insanity, the ruin of the great cities, not mourning the collapse of Western civilization but turning back for her inspiration to prehistory, to a gynocentric tradition. H.D. insisted that the poet-as-woman should stop pouring her energies into a ground left sterile by the power-mongers and death-cultists: "Let us leave/ the place-of-a-skull/ to them that have made it." Nor did we know that H.D.'s life had been literally saved by a woman, Bryher, who took her off to Greece after her near death in childbirth in the 1917 flu epidemic, and stood beside her while the poet underwent the hallucination, or vision, out of which her mature work was to flower. For women, the "break-down" of Western "civilization" between the wars and after the holocaust, has never seemed as ultimate and consequential as it has for men; Lillian Smith remarks in an essay[*] that

*"On Women's Autobiography" in *Generations: Women in the South,* Special issue of *Southern Exposure,* Vol. IV No. 1, Winter 1977.

what Freud "mistook for her lack of civilization is woman's lack of *loyalty* to civilization". What the male poets were mourning and despairing over had never *been* ours, and, as H.D. saw, what we have yet to create does not depend on their institutions; would in fact rather be free of them. She saw that for her as a woman poet, "the walls do not fall" — there are living sources for her that transcend the death-spiral of patriarchy. Judy Grahn is a direct inheritor of that passion for life in the woman poet, that instinct for true power, not domination, which poets like Barrett Browning, Dickinson, H.D., were asserting in their own very different ways and voices.

The last section in this book, "Confrontations With the Devil in the Form of Love" are astringent, low-key, variations on the theme of love as personal solution, salvation, false control, false power. Some of them have the acid taste of wild apples, the sting of the unforgettable, as:

> Love came along and saved
> no one
> Love came along, went broke
> got busted, was run out of
> town and desperately needs—
> something. Dont tell her it's Love.

I find myself wishing I could see these "confrontations" inscribed every which-way on a wall—not hung together in linear sequence—for each takes on new meaning read with the others, and the apparently innocent and casual in Grahn's work is often the most subversive, ironic, and shrewd. The "devil " is always that which wants us to settle for less than we deserve, for panaceas, hand-outs, temporary safety; and for women, the devil has most often taken the form of

20

love rather than of power, gold or learning. So the apparent lightness of these poems had better be taken very seriously, and we might well call to mind, as we read these latest poems the redefinition of "lovers" that Grahn has offered us in "A Woman Is Talking to Death".

The necessity of poetry has to be stated over and over, but only to those who have reason to fear its power, or those who still believe that language is "only words" and that an old language is good enough for our descriptions of the world we are trying to transform.

Adrienne Rich
Montague, Mass.
August 1977

EDWARD THE DYKE
AND OTHER POEMS

1964 ~ 1970

Like most women who write I began to hide it as I grew older, embarrassed that someone might see the scribbled notes in my pockets. By the early 1960's my reasons for hiding notes had become more explicitly political—my subject was women in general, and lesbians in particular. Such notes could be, and sometimes were seized by government authorities and used against other people, as happened to me in the Air Force. I burned my notes more than once. In 1964, the satire which opens this volume was hidden among my notebooks, completely unpublishable. Called *The Psychoanalysis of Edward the Dyke,* it criticizes the mistreatment of women in the hands of the medical profession.

Four years later, in 1969, and in the eye of a new storm of feminism, my lover Wendy Cadden and I helped to found the gay women's liberation movement on the West Coast. We discovered that women love poetry which is true to our own experience, and art which helps us see ourselves without masks. We also found that the independent women's presses are the foundation of women's literature. They have made it possible to speak the unspeakable, to reveal what has had to be hidden, to redefine the experiences of women, and the connections among us.

At 16 I thought that the apex of poetic success would be to appear in the same anthology with Amy Lowell. What has actually happened is infinitely more real.

I called my first, woman-produced, mimeographed book *Edward the Dyke and Other Poems* for two reasons: first, by insisting that *Edward* was a poem, I was telling myself that women must define what our poetry is. I believe this about every other aspect of our lives also. Secondly, it meant people had to say the word *dyke.* What would Amy Lowell say to this? She would probably offer me a cigar.

I'm not a girl
   I'm a hatchet
I'm not a hole
   I'm a whole mountain
I'm not a fool
   I'm a survivor
I'm not a pearl
   I'm the Atlantic Ocean
I'm not a good lay
   I'm a straight razor
look at me as if you had never seen a woman before
I have red, red hands and much bitterness

THE PSYCHOANALYSIS
OF EDWARD THE DYKE

Behind the brown door which bore the gilt letters of Dr. Merlin Knox's name, Edward the Dyke was lying on the doctor's couch which was so luxurious and long that her feet did not even hang over the edge.

"Dr. Knox," Edward began, "my problem this week is chiefly concerning restrooms."

"Aahh," the good doctor sighed. Gravely he drew a quick sketch of a restroom in his notebook.

"Naturally I can't go into men's restrooms without feeling like an interloper, but on the other hand every time I try to use the ladies room I get into trouble."

"Umm," said Dr. Knox, drawing a quick sketch of a door marked 'Ladies'.

"Four days ago I went into the powder room of a department store and three middle-aged housewives came in and thought I was a man. As soon as I explained to them that I was really only a harmless dyke, the trouble began..."

"You compulsively attacked them."

"Oh heavens no, indeed not. One of them turned on the water faucet and tried to drown me with wet paper towels, but the other two began screaming something about how well did I know Gertrude Stein and what sort of underwear did I have on, and they took my new cuff links and socks for souvenirs. They had my head in the trash can and were cutting pieces off my shirttail when luckily a policeman heard my calls for help and rushed in. He was able to divert their attention by shooting at me, thus giving me a chance to escape through the window."

Carefully Dr. Knox noted in his notebook: 'Apparent suicide attempt after accosting girls in restroom.' "My child," he murmured in featherly tones, "have no fear. You must trust us. We will cure you of this deadly affliction, and before you know it you'll be all fluffy and wonderful with dear babies and a bridge club of your very own." He drew a quick sketch of a bridge club. "Now let me see. I believe we estimated that after only four years of intensive therapy and two years of anti-intensive therapy, plus a few minor physical changes and you'll be exactly the little girl we've always wanted you to be." Rapidly Dr. Knox thumbed through an index on his desk. "Yes yes. This year the normal cup size is 56 inches. And waist 12 and ½. Nothing a few well-placed hormones can't accomplish in these advanced times. How tall did you tell me you were?"

"Six feet, four inches," replied Edward.

"Oh, tsk tsk." Dr. Knox did some figuring. "Yes, I'm afraid that will definitely entail extracting approximately 8 inches from each leg, including the knee-cap...standing a lot doesn't bother you, does it my dear?"

"Uh," said Edward, who couldn't decide.

"I assure you the surgeon I have in mind for you is remarkably successful." He leaned far back in his chair. "Now tell me, briefly, what the word 'homosexuality' means to you, in your own words."

"Love flowers pearl, of delighted arms. Warm and water. Melting of vanilla wafer in the pants. Pink petal roses trembling overdew on the lips, soft and juicy fruit. No teeth. No nasty spit. Lips chewing oysters without grimy sand or whiskers. Pastry. Gingerbread. Warm, sweet bread. Cinnamon toast poetry. Justice equality higher wages. Independent angel song. It means I can do what I want."

"Now my dear," Dr. Knox said, "Your disease has gotten

completely out of control. We scientists know of course that it's a highly pleasurable experience to take someone's penis or vagina into your mouth—it's pleasurable and enjoyable. Everyone knows that. But after you've taken a thousand pleasurable penises or vaginas into your mouth and had a thousand people take your pleasurable penis or vagina into their mouth, what have you accomplished? What have you got to show for it? Do you have a wife or children or a husband or a home or a trip to Europe? Do you have a bridge club to show for it? No! You have only a thousand pleasurable experiences to show for it. Do you see how you're missing the meaning of life? How sordid and depraved are these clandestine sexual escapades in parks and restrooms? I ask you."

"But sir but sir," said Edward, "I'm a *woman*. I don't have sexual escapades in parks or restrooms. I don't have a thousand lovers—I have *one* lover."

"Yes yes." Dr. Knox flicked the ashes from his cigar, onto the floor. "Stick to the subject, my dear."

"We were in college then," Edward said. "She came to me out of the silky midnight mist, her slips rustling like cow thieves, her hair blowing in the wind like Gabriel. Lying in my arms harps played soft in dry firelight, Oh Bach. Oh Brahms. Oh Buxtehude. How sweetly we got along how well we got the woods pregnant with canaries and parakeets, barefoot in the grass alas pigeons, but it only lasted ten years and she was gone, poof! like a puff of wheat."

"You see the folly of these brief, physical embraces. But tell me the results of our experiment we arranged for you last session."

"Oh yes. My real date. Well I bought a dress and a wig and a girdle and a squeezy bodice. I did unspeakaï ə things to my armpits with a razor. I had my hair done and my face done and my nails done. My roast done. My bellybutton done."

"And then you felt truly feminine."

"I felt truly immobilized. I could no longer run, walk bend stoop move my arms or spread my feet apart."

"Good, good."

"Well, everything went pretty well during dinner, except my date was only 5'3" and oh yes. One of my eyelashes fell into the soup—that wasn't too bad. I hardly noticed it going down. But then my other eyelash fell on my escort's sleeve and he spent five minutes trying to kill it."

Edward sighed. "But the worst part came when we stood up to go. I rocked back on my heels as I pushed my chair back under the table and my shoes—you see they were three inchers, raising me to 6'7", and with all my weight on those teeny little heels...."

"Yes yes."

"I drove the spikes all the way into the thick carpet and could no longer move. Oh, everyone was nice about it. My escort offered to get the check and to call in the morning to see how I had made out and the manager found a little saw and all. But, Dr. Knox, you must understand that my underwear was terribly binding and the room was hot..."

"Yes yes."

"So I fainted. I didn't *mean* to, I just did. That's how I got my ankles broken."

Dr. Knox cleared his throat. "It's obvious to me, young lady, that you have failed to control your P.E."

"My God," said Edward, glancing quickly at her crotch, "I took a bath just before I came."

29

"This oral eroticism of yours is definitely rooted in Penis Envy, which showed when you deliberately castrated your date by publicly embarrassing him."

Edward moaned. "But strawberries. But lemon cream pie."

"Narcissism," Dr. Knox droned, "Masochism, Sadism. Admit you want to kill your mother."

"Marshmellow bluebird," Edward groaned, eyes softly rolling. "Looking at the stars. April in May."

"Admit you want to possess your father. Mother substitute. Breast suckle."

"Graham cracker subway," Edward writhed, slobbering. "Pussy willow summer."

"Admit you have a smegmatic personality," Dr. Knox intoned.

Edward rolled to the floor. "I am vile! I am vile!"

Dr. Knox flipped a switch at his elbow and immediately a picture of a beautiful woman appeared on a screen over Edward's head. The doctor pressed another switch and electric shocks jolted through her spine. Edward screamed. He pressed another switch, stopping the flow of electricity. Another switch and a photo of a gigantic erect male organ flashed into view, coated in powdered sugar. Dr. Knox handed Edward a lollipop.

She sat up. "I'm saved," she said, tonguing the lollipop.

"Your time is up," Dr. Knox said. "Your check please. Come back next week."

"Yes sir yes sir," Edward said as she went out the brown door. In his notebook, Dr. Knox made a quick sketch of his bank.

I have come to claim
Marilyn Monroe's body
for the sake of my own.
dig it up, hand it over,
cram it in this paper sack.
hubba. hubba. hubba.
look at those luscious
long brown bones, that wide and crusty
pelvis. ha HA, oh she wanted so much to be serious

but she never stops smiling now.
Has she lost her mind?

Marilyn, be serious — they're taking
your picture, and they're taking the pictures
of eight young women in New York City
who murdered themselves for being pretty
by the same method as you, the very
next day, after you!
I have claimed their bodies too,
they smile up out of my paper sack
like brainless cinderellas.

the reporters are furious, they're asking
me questions
what right does a woman have
to Marilyn Monroe's body? and what
am I doing for lunch? They think I
mean to eat you. Their teeth are lurid
and they want to pose me, leaning
on the shovel, nude. Dont squint.

31

But when one of the reporters comes too close
I beat him, bust his camera
with your long, smooth thigh
and with your lovely knucklebone
I break his eye.

Long ago you wanted to write poems;
Be serious, Marilyn
I am going to take you in this paper sack
around the world, and
write on it: — the poems of Marilyn Monroe —
Dedicated to all princes,
the male poets who were so sorry to see you go,
before they had a crack at you.
They wept for you, and also
they wanted to stuff you
while you still had a little meat left
in useful places;
but they were too slow.

Now I shall take them my paper sack
and we shall act out a poem together:
"How would you like to see Marilyn Monroe,
in action, smiling, and without her clothes?"
We shall wait long enough to see them make familiar faces
and then I shall beat them with your skull.
hubba. hubba. hubba. hubba. hubba.
Marilyn, be serious
Today I have come to claim your body for my own.

Elephant Poem

Suppose you have an elephant
with 56 millimeter trunk
and say he's
            tearing up the jungle
(say you think he's drunk
or crazy)
How're you going to bring that elephant down?
lion can't
bear could but don't want to
and the panther's too small for that job.

Then suppose you have an elephant
with million millimeter trunk
and his jungle is the whole green world?
(and drunk
and crazy)
you see the problem.
                    one more word
about elephants
No matter how hard they try
elephants cannot pick their noses
any more than bankers can hand out money
or police put away their pistols
or politicians get right with God.

a sty
in the elephant's eye
aint nothing
but a fly in his nose
is a serious if not fatal condition

when the fly
gets into that nostril
it begins to swell
and stay closed
he can't smell can't drink can't think
can't get one up
on anybody
he begins to regret
all that flabby ammunition
hanging on him
he begins to wish
he'd been a little more bare-faced
like an ape or a fish
all those passageways
he needs to feed himself
tied up

ELEPHANT TURNED UPSIDE DOWN
by a fly
a million flies
outweigh a trunk
a tank
a bank
a million flies
outthink a pile of IBM
junk

we must be wise
to the elephant's lies
you may think we should try
to sober him up
but the trouble isn't that he's drunk
the trouble is
that he's an elephant
with multi-millimeter trunk
who believes the world is his jungle
and until he dies
he grows and grows

we must be flies
in the elephant's nose
ready to carry on
in every town
you know there are butterflies
there are horse flies and house flies
blue flies, shoo flies and it's-not-
true flies
then there are may flies and wood flies
but I'm talking about
can flies & do flies
bottle flies, rock flies and sock flies
dragonflies and fireflies
in the elephant's nose
ready to carry on
til he goes down

If this be/ the banana

take

the banana

take

the banana

Yesterday sucked up its

    following Directions:

if you want to
wet yr chin
take yr face and
stick it

        in

Tomorrow
    aint got no tomorrow.

this is what/I love her

think of it

as silver guppies

in my stomach muscles

pieces of fruit

a day

no other

the harvest spider

flowers on my wall

ornately

legs stretched long and

easy as a young queen

in the park

he knows his trick

will come and meanwhile

he's not asking

In Larry's Room

because it is always possible

the next egg cracked in the pan

will fly off somewhere

we go to Larry's room

unguarded

leave the crosseyed lions in the drive

their thorny paws tucked under

we must pick out

    what hurts us

and discard it.   for a while

in Larry's room we loose un

   structured

dance electrons

               free green

  energy

of all the diatoms at sea

that built us

because it is always possible

we swarm into fish

          and spin

and spawn

until the water is wine is

  white

  ecstatic skin

we drink it

       and a giant leprechaun

becomes the shadow of my body

  on the wall my body is

my own

reflection

if the room shines

as the head of a pin shines then

  it dances

because the exhaled atoms

of my breath are

   me still

I live everywhere   possible

breathing swordfish and lions and

Larry

   wearing Merlin's hat

breaks an egg and holds the

shell close to his ear

the 7 oceans listen

and begin to roar

and roar

and roar

Beside the bench

the tipped milk carton

is orange

the ants line

1

1

1

are not orange

paper clips on the ground

are not orange

waiting to walk away

my foot

is a brown boot with feathers

orange

in the place where
her breasts come together
two thumbs' width of
channel ride my
eyes to anchor
hands to angle
in the place where
her legs come together
I said 'you smell like the
ocean' and lay down my tongue
beside the dark tooth edge
of sleeping
'swim' she told me and I
did, I did

If you lose your lover
rain hurt you. blackbirds
brood over the sky trees
burn down everywhere brown
rabbits run under
car wheels. should your
body cry? to feel such
blue and empty bed dont
bother. if you lose your
lover comb hair go here
or there get   another

Asking for Ruthie

you know her hustle
you know her white legs
flicker among headlights
and her eyes pick up the wind - wink
while the fast hassle of living
ticks off her days
you know her ways

you know her hustle
you know her lonely pockets empty
lined with tricks filled by prostituting
turned and forgotten
the men like (mice) hide
under her mind
lumpy, bigeyed - diff.
you know her pride

you know her blonde arms cut
by broken nickels in
hotelrooms and by razors of
summer lightning on the road
but you know the wizard
highway, no resisting so
she moves, she is forever missing

get her a stopping place
before the night slides dirty
fingers under her eyelids and
the weight of much bad kissing
breaks that ricepaper face

sun cover her, earth
make love to Ruthie
stake her to hot lunches in the wheat fields
make bunches of purple ravens
fly out in formation, over her eyes
and let her newest lovers
be gentle as women
and longer lasting

one white tree branch
wrapped in bird toes
five crows sleeping

Vietnamese woman speaking
to an American soldier

Stack your body
on my body
make
        life
make children play
in my jungle hair
make rice flare into my sky like
whitest flak
the whitest flash
my eyes have
        burned out
looking
press your swelling weapon
here
between us   if you
push it quickly I should
    come
to understand your purpose
what you bring us
what you call it
there
in your country

detroit

that old lady who
lived in shoes
remember, over
breeding, under
feeding her
toe children
crammed together
in the stinking
footgear she, she
burned it all down
yesterday her
shoe my
shoe anybody's
old black shoe

why do Americans
hate to sit next to each other
if you have 8 park benches and
18 people
10 will stand up
10 will stand up and stare past the pigeons
who never sit by themselves
1 ant plus
another ant make a community but
200 million Americans   make one large ant eater
climbing up to the sandia caves I
thought about our ancestors
how scruffy and strong their
toes must have been, to scrabble in those rocks
I cannot do anything with my toes
even fingers grow only on harpsichordists

we have already forgotten
what mattered about them
the anthropologists who stripped the caves
of all nonessentials
being unable to ressurect
their simplicity and their
joy
make busy diagrams of bones and broken dishes

did they go barefoot in the snow
did it burn them
I believe
they held onto each other with their toes
we are not allowed to go barefoot
it is no longer allowed to be snowing

there was a time the dead looked
dead
you could tell them from the living
a man who began to perish in those caves
need not wait half a century for it to finish
there is something to be said for not living
indefinitely
nowadays a man who puts a bullet into his head
is liable to be breathing 10 years later
suckled with needles and tubes
and the clinical curiosity of strangers
there was no capsule in that time
to protect them from love or violence
and if a neighboring tribesman
zonked you on the head and
ate your brains
it was a meaningful sacrifice
you would have done the same
nobody I know has tried to eat a medal of honor

I would crawl up the cliff face to meet the old people
but I having died 7 times already
except for the grace of
penicillin
should have been laid long ago
on the rimrock
to burn in the snow
they had no need for childless women
as we have not much need for mothers
what we need are more park benches
and fewer pigeons
who do not sit by themselves

we who have no darkness
to build fires in
shall go on lopping off the animal parts
we cannot use any more
until we are all shaped like craniums
God will notice the world rolling
with eggs
who cannot reproduce themselves
my ancestors
I would crawl up the cliff face
to meet you
but my toes are misshapen
we are all born with shoes on

the centipede's poem

I never asked the reason
some are yellow owls
and some howl
I never asked an accounting of legs
or heart chambers
we walked out of the sea
on whatever we had to walk on
and some stayed in
there is every kind of animal
that there is
and neither the moon nor the man nor
the mango tree
answers it
I never asked why mice in a woodpile
were not me
I eat whatever I
eat go where I go and
sit quite still
breathing

fortunately the skins

peel back to let

us in

feelings of pulp moving

under the mouth who finds

how sweet to be

how blonde your

hips fit

I kiss your

ears your blood

bangs into my

love my life

beats

sing it

fortunately the skins shout

tambourine speeches

we understand

brush of your hair in

my ears who find your

belly a white drum thumping

snare to come upon how

blonde you are

I suck your

lips your teeth

bite into my

life my red love

take it

A History of Lesbianism

How they came into the world,
the women-loving-women
came in three by three
and four by four
the women-loving-women
came in ten by ten
and ten by ten again
until there were more
than you could count

    they took care of each other
    the best they knew how
    and of each other's children,
    if they had any.

How they lived in the world,
the women-loving-women
learned as much as they were allowed
and walked and wore their clothes
the way they liked
whenever they could. They did whatever
they knew to be happy or free
and worked and worked and worked.
The women-loving-women
in America were called dykes
and some liked it
and some did not.

they made love to each other
the best they knew how
and for the best reasons

How they went out of the world,
the women-loving-women
went out one by one
having withstood greater and lesser
trials, and much hatred
from other people, they went out
one by one, each having tried
in her own way to overthrow
the rule of men over women,
they tried it one by one
and hundred by hundred,
until each came in her own way
to the end of her life
and died.

The subject of lesbianism
is very ordinary; it's the question
of male domination that makes everybody
angry.

one August morning

the mockingbird announced

that the night rains

had driven up

a thousand easy worms

and drowned all the cats

on earth

the big horse woman
walked out to the mountain
it was early in the morning
nobody was around

she was carrying a blanket
and she spread it on the ground
she sat down hard upon it
and made a moaning sound

the mountain wind was blowing
and she shuddered once or twice
as she pressed down on her belly
that was cold, and blue as ice

red was above the mountain
and red was in her eyes
and red the water running
on the big horse woman's thighs

a herd of speckled ponies
came up the hill behind
with four mares at the head
and two horse colts behind

and when she stood up finally
she smiled like a rising sun
and whatever she had on her mind
she didn't tell no one

this poem is called
how Naomi gets her period

THE COMMON WOMAN

1969

The Common Woman Poems have more than fulfilled my idealistic expectations of art as a useful subject—of art as a doer, rather than a passive object to be admired. All by themselves they went around the country. Spurred by the enthusiasm of women hungry for realistic pictures, they were reprinted hundreds of thousands of times, were put to music, danced, used to name various women's projects, quoted and then misquoted in a watered-down fashion for use on posters and T-shirts.

Their origin was completely practical: I wanted, in 1969, to read something which described regular, everyday women without making us look either superhuman or pathetic. The closest I could come to finding such an image was a Leonard Cohen song about a whimsical woman named Suzanne, who takes you down to her place by the river. This was on an album of Nina Simone's, and I played that song numberless times during the night I wrote the seven portraits. Oddly, although the song is not a waltz, the poems are. (Try reading them while someone else hums a waltz.) I conceived of them as flexible, self-defining sonnets, seeing that each woman would let me know how many lines were needed to portray her in one long, informative thought.

I paid particular attention to ways of linking them together, and of connecting the facts of their lives with images which called up various natural powers, hoping that these combinations would help break current stereotypes about women and the work we do. I wanted to accentuate the strengths of their persons without being false about the facts of their lives. To admire them for what they are, already. I still do.

women hungry for realistic pictures

60

I. Helen, at 9 am, at noon, at 5:15

Her ambition is to be more shiny
and metallic, black and purple as
a thief at midday; trying to make it
in a male form, she's become as
stiff as possible. — hand on
Wearing trim suits and spike heels,
she says "bust" instead of breast;
somewhere underneath she
misses love and trust, but she feels
that spite and malice are the   male value
prices of success. She doesn't realize
yet, that she's missed success, also,
so her smile is sometimes still
genuine. After a while she'll be a real
killer, bitter and more wily, better at
pitting the men against each other   mentar ness
and getting the other women fired.
She constantly conspires.
Her grief expresses itself in fits of fury
over details, details take the place of meaning,
money takes the place of life.
She believes that people are lice
who eat her, so she bites first; her
thirst increases year by year and by the time
the sheen has disappeared from her black hair,
and tension makes her features unmistakably
ugly, she'll go mad. No one in particular
will care. As anyone who's had her for a boss
will know
the common woman is as common
as the common crow.

II. Ella, in a square apron, along Highway 80

She's a copperheaded waitress,
tired and sharp-worded, she hides
her bad brown tooth behind a wicked
smile, and flicks her ass
out of habit, to fend off the pass
that passes for affection.
She keeps her mind the way men
keep a knife — keen to strip the game
down to her size. She has a thin spine, *manliness*
swallows her eggs cold, and tells lies.
She slaps a wet rag at the truck drivers,
if they should complain. She understands
the necessity for pain, turns away
the smaller tips, out of pride, and
keeps a flask under the counter. Once,
she shot a lover who misused her child.
Before she got out of jail, the courts had pounced
and given the child away. Like some isolated lake,
her flat blue eyes take care of their own stark
bottoms. Her hands are nervous, curled, ready
to scrape.
The common woman is as common
as a rattlesnake.

not sanatized language.

III. Nadine, resting on her neighbor's stoop

She holds things together, collects bail,
makes the landlord patch the largest holes.
At the Sunday social she would spike   *masculinity)*
every drink, and offer you half of what she knows,
which is plenty. She pokes at the ruins of the city
like an armored tank; but she thinks
of herself as a ripsaw cutting through
knots in wood. Her sentences come out
like thick pine shanks
and her big hands fill the air like smoke.
She's a mud-chinked cabin in the slums,
sitting on the doorstep counting
rats and raising 15 children,
half of them her own. The neighborhood
would burn itself out without her;
one of these days she'll strike the spark herself.
She's made of grease
and metal, with a hard head
that makes the men around her seem frail.
The common woman is as common as
a nail.

IV. Carol, in the park, chewing on straws

　　　　She has taken a woman lover
　　　　whatever shall we do
　　　　she has taken a woman lover
　　　　how lucky it wasnt you
And all the day through she smiles and lies
and grits her teeth and pretends to be shy,
or weak, or busy. Then she goes home
and pounds her own nails, makes her own
bets, and fixes her own car, with her friend.
She goes as far
as women can go without protection
from men.
On weekends, she dreams of becoming a tree;
a tree that dreams it is ground up
and sent to the paper factory, where it
lies helpless in sheets, until it dreams
of becoming a paper airplane, and rises
on its own current; where it turns into a
bird, a great coasting bird that dreams of becoming
more free, even, than that — a feather, finally, or
a piece of air with lightning in it.

　　　　she has taken a woman lover
　　　　whatever can we say
She walks around all day
quietly, but underneath it
she's electric;
angry energy inside a passive form.
The common woman is as common
as a thunderstorm.

67

V. Detroit Annie, hitchhiking

Her words pour out as if her throat were a broken
artery and her mind were cut-glass, carelessly handled.
You imagine her in a huge velvet hat with great
dangling black feathers,
but she shaves her head instead
and goes for three-day midnight walks.
Sometimes she goes down to the dock and dances
off the end of it, simply to prove her belief
that people who cannot walk on water
are phonies, or dead.
When she is cruel, she is very, very
cool and when she is kind she is lavish.
Fishermen think perhaps she's a fish, but they're all
fools. She figured out that the only way
to keep from being frozen was to
stay in motion, and long ago converted
most of her flesh into liquid. Now when she
smells danger, she spills herself all over,
like gasoline, and lights it.
She leaves the taste of salt and iron
under your tongue, but you dont mind
The common woman is as common
as the reddest wine.

VI. Margaret, seen through a picture window

After she finished her first abortion
she stood for hours and watched it spinning in the
toilet, like a pale stool.
Some distortion of the rubber
doctors with their simple tubes and
complicated prices,
still makes her feel guilty.
White and yeasty.
All her broken bubbles push her down
into a shifting tide, where her own face
floats above her like the whole globe.
She lets her life go off and on
in a slow strobe.
At her last job she was fired for making
strikes, and talking out of turn;
now she stays home, a little blue around the edges.
Counting calories and staring at the empty
magazine pages, she hates her shape
and calls herself overweight.
Her husband calls her a big baboon.
Lusting for changes, she laughs through her
teeth, and wanders from room to room.
The common woman is as solemn as a monkey
or a new moon.

VII. Vera, from my childhood

Solemnly swearing, to swear as an oath to you
who have somehow gotten to be a pale old woman;
swearing, as if an oath could be wrapped around
your shoulders
like a new coat:
For your 28 dollars a week and the bastard boss
you never let yourself hate;
and the work, all the work you did at home
where you never got paid;
For your mouth that got thinner and thinner
until it disappeared as if you had choked on it,
watching the hard liquor break your fine husband down
into a dead joke.
For the strange mole, like a third eye
right in the middle of your forehead;
for your religion which insisted that people
are beautiful golden birds and must be preserved;
for your persistent nerve
and plain white talk—
the common woman is as common
as good bread
as common as when you couldnt go on
but did.
For all the world we didnt know we held in common
all along
the common woman is as common as the best of bread
and will rise
and will become strong — I swear it to you
I swear it to you on my own head
I swear it to you on my common
woman's
head

SHE WHO

1971 ~ 1972

The She Who poems passed my critical judgment when each was able to set my own teeth on edge. I like best those which take linguistic risks—especially *the most blonde woman.*

The two back-to-back *Plainsongs* are sisters, and very different. The form for *Plainsong* Number One happened after a dictionary informed me that there are two kinds of rhymes, masculine and feminine. Masculine rhymes, the explanation said, are one syllable, important, serious, like *man, can, ran.* There was a long list of them. Feminine rhymes were characterized as two-syllable, unimportant, used only for humor, not worth listing. I began making my own listings of feminine rhymes, such as *forming, swarming,* etc. I became even more fascinated remembering that Chaucerian Old English contained many feminine rhymes in words such as *take´* and *make´,* presently pronounced as masculine rhymes.

The second *Plainsong* is not a poem at all, it is a funeral ritual, and has been used at memorials a number of times. In such ways we begin to reclaim the events of our own lives, as well as making our poetry what it should be and once was: specific, scientific, valuable, of real use.

The ending List of universal qualities in women is based in a great deal of fact. *The woman whose head is on fire,* for instance, is someone I met who later burned herself up in protest over the War in Vietnam. And *the woman with the tatoo of a bird,* was originally a person fresh out of the Navy who had a magnificent, three-colored seahorse on her shoulderblade. Seahorse did not scan well in the line, so I made it a bird. Later, a woman ran up to me after a reading, dropped her trousers, pointed accusingly to a small blue bird tatooed on her thigh, and said, "How did you know?" Aha, so now you see. She Who knows everything.

She Who
She, she SHE, she SHE, she WHO?
she - she WHO she - WHO she WHO - SHE?
She, she who? she WHO? she, WHO SHE?

who who SHE, she - who, she WHO - WHO?
she WHO - who, WHO - who, WHO - who, WHO - who.....

She. who - WHO, she WHO. She WHO - who SHE?
who she SHE, who SHE she, SHE - who WHO—
She WHO?
She SHE who, She, she SHE
she SHE, she SHE who.
<u>SHEEE</u>   <u>WHOOOOOO</u>

She Who continues.
She Who has a being
named She Who is a being
named She Who carries her own name.
She Who turns things over.
She Who marks her own way, gathering.
She Who makes her own difference.
She Who differs, gathering her own events.
She Who gathers, gaining
She Who carries her own ways,
gathering She Who waits,
bearing She Who cares for her
own name, carrying She Who
bears, gathering She Who cares
for She Who gathers her own ways,
carrying
the names of She Who gather and gain,
singing: I am the woman, the woman
            the woman - I am the first person.
and the first person is She Who is the first person to
She Who is the first person to no other. There is no
other first person.

She Who floods like a river and
like a river continues
She Who continues

The wolf spider is a creature of striking
habits. Although she has eight legs and many eyes
like other spiders, her body tends to be thick
and more hairy, and she does not spin a web and
wait for her quarry to be caught. Instead, wolf
spiders hunt in packs, their usual prey being
the big green praying mantis. The wolf spiders
surround the mantis or drive it over a cliff, and
then beat it to death with tiny pebbles. After
ward, they carefully dismember the body, and
carry it home to cook.

Sheep

The first four leaders had broken knees
The four old dams had broken knees
The flock would start to run, then freeze
The first four leaders had broken knees

'Why is the flock so docile?' asked the hawk.
'Yes, why *is* the flock so docile,' laughed the dog,

'The shepherd's mallet is in his hand,
The shepherd's hand is on the land,
The flock will start to run, then freeze--
The four old dams have broken knees,'
The dog explained.

The hawk exclaimed:
'The shepherd leads an easy life!'

'I know, I know,' cried the shepherd's wife,
'He dresses me out in a narrow skirt
and leaves me home to clean his dirt.
Whenever I try to run, I freeze--
All the old dams have broken knees.'

'Well, I'm so glad he doesnt dare
to bring his breaking power to bear
on *me*,' said the hawk, flying into the sun;
while the dog warned, in his dog run:
'Hawk-- the shepherd has bought a gun!'

- - - - -

'Why is the hawk so docile?' asked the flock,

'He fell to the ground in a feathery breeze;
He lies in a dumb lump under the trees.
We believe we'd rather have broken knees
Than lose our blood and suddenly freeze--
like him.'

But the oldest dam gave her leg a lick,
And said, 'Some die slow and some die quick,
A few run away and the rest crawl,
But the shepherd never dies at all--
Damn his soul.
I'd will my wool to the shepherd's wife
If she could change the shepherd's life,
But I myself would bring him low
If only, *only* I knew how.'

parting on the left,
parting on the right,
braiding.

She Who increases
what can be done

I shall grow another breast
in the middle of my chest
what shall it be

not like the other ones lying there
those two fried eggs.

in the center of my flesh
I shall grow another breast
rounder than a ready fist,
slippery as a school of fish,
sounder than stone. Call it
She - Who - educates - my - chest.

She Who.

She is not my daughter, not my son
I'm going to groom her with my tongue
needle her senses with my pain
feed her hunches with my brain,

She Who defends me.

Breast number one
belongs to some, and
breast number two
belongs to you, and
breast number three
is She - Who - works - for - me

Now I have a longer tongue
and three good breasts, and some have none.
what can be done

The enemies of She Who call her various names

a whore, a whore,
a fishwife a cunt a harlot a harlot a pussy
a doxie a tail a fishwife a whore a hole a slit
a cunt a bitch a slut a slit a hole a whore a hole
a vixen/ a piece of ass/ a dame - filly - mare
dove - cow - pig - chick - cat - kitten - bird
dog - dish/   a dumb blonde

you black bitch - you white bitch - you brown bitch - you
yellow bitch - you fat bitch - you stupid bitch - you stinking
bitch you little bitch - you old bitch - a cheap bitch - a high
class bitch - a 2 bit whore - a 2 dollar whore - a ten dollar
whore - a million dollar mistress

a hole a slut a cunt a slit a cut
a slash a hole a slit a piece
of shit, a piece of shit, a piece of shit

She Who bears it
bear down, breathe
bear down, bear down, breathe
bear down, bear down, bear down, breathe

She Who lies down in the darkness and bears it
She Who lies down in the lightness and bears it
the labor of She Who carries and bears is the first labor

all over the world
the waters are breaking everywhere
everywhere the waters are breaking
the labor of She Who carries and bears
and raises and rears is the first labor,
there is no other first labor.

The many minnows are fishes that live in a stream,
and greedybeak is a bird that lives on the land
and comes down to the edge of the stream where he
sticks his head under the water and eats the
many minnows. After a long time of this greedybeak
had ate up all but 47 of the many minnows and they
were tired of it so the next time he approached
their stream they had a plan. They thrust all of their
silver scales and fins out as far as they would
go, and all in the same direction. The sun's rays
glinted off the silver scales and fins, and when
greedybeak looked down he saw nothing but his
own reflection. "Theres another greedybeak down
there with MY fishes" he screamed and dove
straight into the water, in a rage. The 47
remaining many minnows promptly ate him up
and turned him into many more many minnows.

She Who,
She Who carries herself in a bowl of blood
She Who holds a bowl of blood
and swallows a speck of foam
She Who molds her blood in a bowl
in a bowl, in a bowl of blood
and the bowl, and the bowl and the blood
and the foam and the bowl, and the bowl
and the blood belong to She Who holds it.

She shook it till it got some shape.
She shook it the first season and lost some teeth
She shook it the second season and lost some bone
She shook it the third season and some body was born,
She Who.

A Geology Lesson

Here, the sea strains to climb up on the land
and the wind blows dust in a single direction.
The trees bend themselves all one way
and volcanoes explode often
Why is this? Many years back
a woman of strong purpose
passed through this section
and everything else tried to follow.

The woman in three pieces -- one

She said she was unhappy and they said they would take care of her. She said she needed love and so they raped her and then she wanted to be alone. They locked her into a tiny cell with one tiny window and took away her clothes, turning off all the lights as they left. After a long while they came back and she said, "It's so dark", so they shined a very bright light into her face and she said "I don't like that". "What's the matter" they said and she said "There is nothing to eat, couldn't you please give me some water" so they brought a hose and sprayed her hard with water. "Are you happy now" they said and she answered "Please, I'm so very cold, my bones ache and I shiver all the time." So they brought huge piles of sticks and newspaper and built a very large fire in her cell. She squeezed her body out of the window and fell a great distance and was killed. "The trouble with people like her" they said later "is that no matter how hard you try to please them, they are never satisfied."

The woman in three pieces — two

We said we were unhappy and they said they would take care of us. We needed love, they said, and so they raped us, and then they wanted to be alone. They locked us into a little cell with one tiny window and took away our clothes, turning off all the lights as they left. After a long while they came back and we said "It's so dark" so they shined a very bright light into our faces and we said "We don't really like that." "What's the matter" they said and we said "Well, there is nothing to eat, couldn't you please give us some water" so they brought a hose and sprayed us hard with water. "Are you happy now" they said and we answered "Please, we would be, but we're so very cold, our bones ache and we shiver all the time". So they brought huge piles of sticks and newspaper and built a very large fire in our cell. We squeezed our bodies out of the tiny window and fell a great distance and were killed. "The trouble with people like them" they said later among themselves, "is that no matter how hard they try to please us, we are never satisfied."

The woman in three pieces — three

I said I was unhappy and you said I would take care of him.
I needed love, he said, and so he raped you and then everyone
wanted to be alone.

We locked ourselves into a little cell with one tiny window
and took away our clothes, turning off all the lights as we
left.

After along time we came back and I said "It's so dark" so
we shined a bright light into his face and you said "He
doesnt like that."

"What's the matter" I said and you said "There is nothing
to eat, couldnt you please give him some water?" So we
brought a hose and sprayed me hard with water.

"Are you happy now" I said and he answered, "Please, you
are so very cold, my bones ache and I shiver all the time."

So you brought huge piles of sticks and newspapers and he
built a very large fire in our cell.

You squeezed my body out of the window and we fell a
great distance and were killed.

"The trouble with people like us" we said later, "is that
no matter how hard I try to please you, I am never satisfied."

She Who sits making a first fire
while the goat watches

a knife, a goat, a blue stone
pound, reflect, flint, reflect
the meal, the morning
the grinding of corn,
slitting
the yellow eyes of the goat
follow and follow
a knife, reflecting
a blue stone
pitted
a scraper, a goat, a yellow stone
straw and the wind, reflect
grind
fold and unfolding a goat's eyes
the morning, the flint, the curved smoke
grinding the jaws of the goat closed
pound, reflect
a knife, a labor, a blue stone
glinting behind the yellow eyes
swallow
the throat of the goat knows
a stone striking a blue stone
blowing, reflect
a grinder, a straw, a red stone
follows, a roast goat follows
a red stone

The most blonde woman in the world
one day threw off her skin
her hair, threw off her hair, declaring
'Whosoever chooses to love me
chooses to love a bald woman
with bleeding pores.'
Those who came then as her lovers
were small hard-bodied spiders
with dark eyes and an excellent
knowledge of weaving.
They spun her blood into long strands,
and altogether wove millions of red
webs, webs red in the afternoon sun.
'Now', she said, 'Now I am expertly loved,
and now I am beautiful.'

She Whose skin is luminous, bluish white,
took a walk outside in the middle of the night.
Her dog howled and howled inside her room;
he thought her face in the window was the moon.

She Whose skin is pitted with tiny holes
filled them up with microscopic moles,
who multiplied so quickly she was led
to fill them up with prairie dogs instead.

Carol and
her crescent wrench
work bench
wooden fence
wide stance
Carol and her
pipe wrench
pipe smoke
pipe line
high climb
smoke eyes
chicken wire
Carol and her
hack saw
well worn
torn back
bad spine
never - mind
timberline
clear mind
Carol and her
hard glance
stiff dance
clean pants
bad ass
lumberjack's
wood ax

Carol and her
big son
shot gun
lot done
not done
never bored
do more
do less
try to rest
Carol and her
new lands
small hands
big plans
Carol and her
long time
out shine
worm gear
warm beer
quick tears
dont stare
Carol is another
queer
chickadee
like me, but Carol does
everything
better
if you let her.

I am the wall at the lip of the water
I am the rock that refused to be battered
I am the dyke in the matter, the other
I am the wall with the womanly swagger
I am the dragon, the dangerous dagger
I am the bulldyke, the bulldagger

and I have been many a wicked grandmother
and I shall be many a wicked daughter.

foam on the rim of the glass
another wave breaking

foam on the rim of the glass
another wave breaking
she once wanted to be a sailor

now she sits at the bar, drinking
like a sailor

a funeral
plainsong from a younger woman to an older woman

i will be your mouth now, to do your singing
breath belongs to those who do the breathing.
warm life, as it passes through your fingers
flares up in the very hands you will be leaving

you have left, what is left
for the bond between women is a circle
we are together within it.

i am your best, i am your kind
kind of my kind, i am your wish
wish of my wish, i am your breast
breast of my breast, i am your mind
mind of my mind, i am your flesh
i am your kind, i am your wish
kind of my kind, i am your best

now you have left you can be
wherever the fire is when it blows itself out.
now you are a voice in any wind
        i am a single wind
now you are any source of a fire
        i am a single fire

wherever you go to, i will arrive
whatever i have been, you will come back to
wherever you leave off, i will inherit
whatever i resurrect, you shall have it

you have right, what is right
for the bond between women is returning
we are endlessly within it
and endlessly apart within it.
it is not finished
it will not be finished

i will be your heart now, to do your loving
love belongs to those who do the feeling.

life, as it stands so still along your fingers
beats in my hands, the hands i will, believing
that you have become she, who is not, any longer
somewhere in particular

we are together in your stillness
you have wished us a bonded life

love of my love, i am your breast
arm of my arm, i am your strength
breath of my breath, i am your foot
thigh of my thigh, back of my back
eye of my eye, beat of my beat
kind of my kind, i am your best

when you were dead i said you had gone to the mountain

the trees do not yet speak of you

a mountain when it is no longer
a mountain, goes to the sea
when the sea dies it goes to the rain
when the rain dies it goes to the grain
when the grain dies it goes to the flesh
when the flesh dies it goes to the mountain

now you have left, you can wander
will you tell whoever could listen
tell all the voices who speak to younger women
tell all the voices who speak to us when we need it
that the love between women is a circle
and is not finished

wherever i go to, you will arrive
whatever you have been, i will come back to
wherever i leave off, you will inherit
whatever we resurrect, we shall have it
we shall have it, we have right

and you have left, what is left

i will take your part now, to do your daring
lots belong to those who do the sharing.
i will be your fight now, to do your winning
as the bond between women is beginning
in the middle at the end
my first beloved, present friend
if i could die like the next rain
i'd call you by your mountain name
and rain on you

want of my want, i am your lust
wave of my wave, i am your crest
earth of my earth, i am your crust
may of my may, i am your must
kind of my kind, i am your best

tallest mountain least mouse
least mountain tallest mouse

you have put your very breath upon mine
i shall wrap my entire fist around you
i can touch any woman's lip to remember

we are together in my motion
you have wished us a bonded life

a funeral: for my first lover and longtime friend
Yvonne Mary Robinson b. Oct. 20, 1939; d. Nov. 1974
for ritual use only

Slowly: a plainsong from an older
woman to a younger woman

am I not   olden olden olden
it is unwanted.

wanting, wanting
am I not   broken
stolen   common

am I not crinkled cranky poison
am I not glinty - eyed and frozen

am I not   aged
shaky   glazing
am I not   hazy
guarded   craven

am I not   only
stingy   little
am I not   simple
brittle   spitting

was I not   over
over   ridden?

it is a long story
will you be proud to be my version?

it is unwritten.

writing, writing
am I not   ancient
raging   patient

am I not   able
charming   stable
was I not   building
forming   braving

was I not   ruling
guiding   naming
was I not   brazen
crazy   chosen

even the stones would do my bidding?

it is a long story
am I not proud to be your version?

it is unspoken.

speaking, speaking
am I not   elder
berry
brandy

are you not wine before you find me
in your own beaker?

do you not turn away your shoulder?
have I not shut my mouth against you?

are you not shamed to treat me meanly
when you discover you become me?
are you not proud that you become me?

I will not shut my mouth against you.
do you not turn away your shoulder.
we who brew in the same bitters
that boil us away
we both need stronger water.

we're touched by a similar nerve.

I am new like your daughter.
I am the will, and the riverbed
made bolder
by you — my oldest river —
you are the way.

are we not   olden, olden, olden.

the woman whose head is on fire
the woman with a noisy voice
the woman with too many fingers
the woman who never smiled once in her life
the woman with a boney body
the woman with moles all over her

the woman who cut off her breast
the woman with a large bobbing head
the woman with one glass eye
the woman with broad shoulders
the woman with callused elbows
the woman with a sunken chest   *mosaic*
the woman who is part giraffe

the woman with five gold teeth
the woman who looks straight ahead
the woman with enormous knees
the woman who can lick her own clitoris
the woman who screams on the trumpet
the woman whose toes grew together
the woman who says I am what I am

the woman with rice under her skin
the woman who owns a machete
the woman who plants potatoes
the woman who murders the kangaroo
the woman who stuffs clothing into a sack
the woman who makes a great racket
the woman who fixes machines
the woman whose chin is sticking out
the woman who says I will be

the woman who carries laundry on her head
the woman who is part horse
the woman who asks so many questions
the woman who cut somebody's throat

the woman who gathers peaches
the woman who carries jars on her head
the woman who howls
the woman whose nose is broken
the woman who constructs buildings
the woman who has fits on the floor
the woman who makes rain happen
the woman who refuses to menstruate

the woman who sets broken bones
the woman who sleeps out on the street
the woman who plays the drums
the woman who is part grasshopper
the woman who herds cattle
the woman whose will is unbending
the woman who hates kittens

the woman who escaped from the jailhouse
the woman who is walking across the desert
the woman who buries the dead
the woman who taught herself writing
the woman who skins rabbits
the woman who believes her own word
the woman who chews bearskin
the woman who eats cocaine
the woman who thinks about everything

the woman who has the tatoo of a bird
the woman who puts things together
the woman who squats on her haunches
the woman whose children are all different   colors

singing   i am the will of the woman
               the woman
               my will is unbending

when She-Who-moves-the-earth will turn over
when She Who moves, the earth will turn over.

A WOMAN IS TALKING TO DEATH

1973

Once a woman poet begins telling the truth there is no end of possibilities. This poem is as factual as I could possibly make it—literary permission which was granted to me at the time by the work of Pat Parker and Alta in some of their poetry and Sharon Isabell in her striking novel, *Yesterday's Lessons.*

The range of effects it has on other people continually astonishes me. It has made drunken women pound the table protesting having to listen, and mature men break down publicly in tears, temporarily unable to function. It has often made large groups of women feel strong and in agreement. For myself, I have grown considerably more determined by having to live up to the poem's forcefulness as well as its commitments, and other people have expressed similar reactions. Pat Parker, who used it as a model for her stunning and much more specific poem, *Womanslaughter,* understood it before I did. It is odd to think that what we make leads us, rather than the other way around.

One characteristic of workingclass writing is that we often pile up many events within a small amount of space rather than detailing the many implications of one or two events. This means both that our lives are chock full of action and also that we are bursting with stories which haven't been printed, made into novels, dictionaries, philosophies.

The particular challenges of this poem for me were how to discuss the criss-cross oppressions which people use against each other and which continually divide us—and how to define a lesbian life within the context of other people in the world. I did not realize at the time that I was also taking up the subject of heroes in a modern life which for many people is more like a war than not, or that I would begin a redefinition for myself of the subject of love.

A Woman Is Talking To Death

One
Testimony in trials that never got heard

my lovers teeth are white geese flying above me
my lovers muscles are rope ladders under my hands

we were driving home slow
my lover and I, across the long Bay Bridge,
one February midnight, when midway
over in the far left lane, I saw a strange scene:

one small young man standing by the rail,
and in the lane itself, parked straight across
as if it could stop anything, a large young
man upon a stalled motorcycle, perfectly
relaxed as if he'd stopped at a hamburger stand;
he was wearing a peacoat and levis, and
he had his head back, roaring, you
could almost hear the laugh, it
was so real.

"Look at that fool," I said, "in the
middle of the bridge like that," a very
womanly remark.

Then we heard the meaning of the noise
of metal on a concrete bridge at 50
miles an hour, and the far left lane
filled up with a big car that had a
motorcycle jammed on its front bumper, like
the whole thing would explode, the friction
sparks shot up bright orange for many feet

into the air, and the racket still sets
my teeth on edge.

When the car stopped we stopped parallel
and Wendy headed for the callbox while I
ducked across those 6 lanes like a mouse
in the bowling alley. "Are you hurt?" I said,
the middle-aged driver had the greyest black face,
"I couldn't stop, I couldn't stop, what happened?"

Then I remembered. "Somebody," I said, "was *on*
the motorcycle." I ran back,
one block? two blocks? the space for walking
on the bridge is maybe 18 inches, whoever
engineered this arrogance. in the dark
stiff wind it seemed I would
be pushed over the rail, would fall down
screaming onto the hard surface of
the bay, but I did not, I found the tall young man
who thought he owned the bridge, now lying on
his stomach, head cradled in his broken arm.

He had glasses on, but somewhere he had lost
most of his levis, where were they?
and his shoes. Two short cuts on his buttocks,
that was the only mark except his thin white
seminal tubes were all strung out behind; no
child left *in* him; and he looked asleep.

I plucked wildly at his wrist, then put it
down; there were two long haired women
holding back the traffic just behind me
with their bare hands, the machines came
down like mad bulls, I was scared, much

more than usual, I felt easily squished
like the earthworms crawling on a busy
sidewalk after the rain; *I wanted to
leave.* And met the driver, walking back.

"The guy is dead." I gripped his hand,
the wind was going to blow us off the bridge.

"Oh my God," he said, "haven't I had enough
trouble in my life?" He raised his head,
and for a second was enraged and yelling,
at the top of the bridge—"I was just driving
home!" His head fell down. "My God, and
now I've killed somebody."

I looked down at my own peacoat and levis,
then over at the dead man's friend, who
was bawling and blubbering, what they would
call hysteria in a woman. "It isn't possible"
he wailed, but it was possible, it was
indeed, accomplished and unfeeling, snoring
in its peacoat, and without its levis on.

He died laughing: that's a fact.

I had a woman waiting for me,
in her car and in the middle of the bridge,
I'm frightened, I said.
I'm afraid, he said, stay with me,
please don't go, stay with me, be
my witness—"No," I said, "I'll be your
witness—later," and I took his name
and number, "but I can't stay with you,

I'm too frightened of the bridge, besides
I have a woman waiting
and no license—
and no tail lights—"
So I left—
as I have left so many of my lovers.

we drove home
shaking, Wendy's face greyer
than any white person's I have ever seen.
maybe he beat his wife, maybe he once
drove taxi, and raped a lover
of mine—how to know these things?
we do each other in, that's a fact.

who will be my witness?
death wastes our time with drunkenness
and depression
death, who keeps us from our
lovers.
he had a woman waiting for him,
I found out when I called the number
days later

"Where is he" she said, "he's disappeared."
He'll be all right" I said, "*we* could
have hit the guy as easy as anybody, it
wasn't anybody's fault, they'll know that,"
women so often say dumb things like that,
they teach us to be sweet and reassuring,
and say ignorant things, because we dont invent
the crime, the punishment, the bridges

that same week I looked into the mirror
and nobody was there to testify;
how clear, an unemployed queer woman
makes no witness at all,
nobody at all was there for
those two questions: what does
she do, and who is she married to?

I am the woman who stopped on the bridge
and this is the man who was there
our lovers teeth are white geese flying
above us, but we ourselves are
easily squished.

keep the women small and weak
and off the street, and off the
bridges, that's the way, brother
one day I will leave you there,
as I have left you there before,
working for death.

we found out later
what we left him to.
Six big policemen answered the call,
all white, and no child *in* them.
they put the driver up against his car
and beat the hell out of him.
What did you kill that poor kid for?
you mutherfucking nigger.
that's a fact.

Death only uses violence
when there is any kind of resistance,

the rest of the time a slow
weardown will do.

They took him to 4 different hospitals
til they got a drunk test report to fit their
case, and held him five days in jail
without a phone call.
how many lovers have we left.

there are as many contradictions to the game,
as there are players.
a woman is talking to death,
though talk is cheap, and life takes a long time
to make
right. He got a cheesy lawyer
who had him cop a plea, 15 to 20
instead of life
Did I say life?

the arrogant young man who thought he
owned the bridge, and fell asleep on it
he died laughing: that's a fact.
the driver sits out his time
off the street somewhere,
does he have the most vacant of
eyes, will he die laughing?

Two
They don't have to lynch the women anymore

death sits on my doorstep
cleaning his revolver

death cripples my feet and sends me out
to wait for the bus alone,
then comes by driving a taxi.

the woman on our block with 6 young children
has the most vacant of eyes
death sits in her bedroom, loading
his revolver

they don't have to lynch the women
very often anymore, although
they used to—the lord and his men
went through the villages at night, beating &
killing every woman caught
outdoors.
the European witch trials took away
the independent people; two different villages
—after the trials were through that year—
had left in them, each—
one living woman:
one

What were those other women up to? had they
run over someone? stopped on the wrong bridge?
did they have teeth like
any kind of geese, or children
in them?

Three
This woman is a lesbian be careful

In the military hospital where I worked
as a nurse's aide, the walls of the halls

were lined with howling women
waiting to deliver
or to have some parts removed.
One of the big private rooms contained
the general's wife, who needed
a wart taken off her nose.
we were instructed to give her special attention
not because of her wart or her nose
but because of her husband, the general.

as many women as men die, and that's a fact.

At work there was one friendly patient, already
claimed, a young woman burnt apart with X-ray,
she had long white tubes instead of openings;
rectum, bladder, vagina—I combed her hair, it
was my job, but she took care of me as if
nobody's touch could spoil her.

ho ho death, ho death
have you seen the twinkle in the dead woman's eye?

when you are a nurse's aide
someone suddenly notices you
and yells about the patient's bed,
and tears the sheets apart so you
can do it over, and over
while the patient waits
doubled over in her pain
for you to make the bed *again*
and no one ever looks at you,
only at what you do not do

Here, general, hold this soldier's bed pan
for a moment, hold it for a year—
then we'll promote you to making his bed.
we believe you wouldn't make such messes

if you had to clean up after them.

that's a fantasy.
this woman is a lesbian, be careful.

When I was arrested and being thrown out
of the military, the order went out: dont anybody
speak to this woman, and for those three
long months, almost nobody did;   the dayroom, when
I entered it, fell silent til I had gone; they
were afraid, they knew the wind would blow
them over the rail, the cops would come,
the water would run into their lungs.
Everything I touched
was spoiled. They were my lovers, those
women, but nobody had taught us to swim.
I drowned, I took 3 or 4 others down
when I signed the confession of what we
had done   together.

No one will ever speak to me again.

I read this somewhere; I wasn't there:
in WW II the US army had invented some floating
amphibian tanks, and took them over to
the coast of Europe to unload them,
the landing ships all drawn up in a fleet,
and everybody watching. Each tank had a

crew of 6 and there were 25 tanks.
The first went down the landing planks
and sank, the second, the third, the
fourth, the fifth, the sixth went down
and sank. They weren't supposed
to sink, the engineers had
made a mistake.   The crews looked around
wildly for the order to quit,
but none came, and in the sight of
thousands of men, each 6 crewmen
saluted his officers, battened down
his hatch in turn and drove into the
sea, and drowned, until all 25 tanks
were gone.   did they have vacant
eyes, die laughing, or what?   what
did they talk about, those men,
as the water came in?

was the general their lover?

Four
A Mock Interrogation

Have you ever held hands with a woman?

Yes, many times—women about to deliver, women about to
have breasts removed, wombs removed, miscarriages, women
having epileptic fits, having asthma, cancer, women having
breast bone marrow sucked out of them by nervous or in-
different interns, women with heart condition, who were
vomiting, overdosed, depressed, drunk, lonely to the point
of extinction: women who had been run over, beaten up.

deserted. starved. women who had been bitten by rats; and women who were happy, who were celebrating, who were dancing with me in large circles or alone, women who were climbing mountains or up and down walls, or trucks or roofs and needed a boost up, or I did; women who simply wanted to hold my hand because they liked me, some women who wanted to hold my hand because they liked me better than anyone.

These were many women?

Yes. many.

What about kissing? Have you kissed any women?

I have kissed many women.

When was the first woman you kissed with serious feeling?

The first woman ever I kissed was Josie, who I had loved at such a distance for months. Josie was not only beautiful, she was tough and handsome too. Josie had black hair and white teeth and strong brown muscles. Then she dropped out of school unexplained. When she came back she came back for one day only, to finish the term, and there was a child in her. She was all shame, pain, and defiance. Her eyes were dark as the water under a bridge and no one would talk to her, they laughed and threw things at her. In the afternoon I walked across the front of the class and looked deep into Josie's eyes and I picked up her chin with my hand, because I loved her, because nothing like her trouble would ever happen to me, because I hated it that she was pregnant and unhappy, and an outcast. We were thirteen.

You didn't kiss her?

How does it feel to be thirteen and having a baby?

You didn't actually kiss her?

Not in fact.

You have kissed other women?

Yes, many, some of the finest women I know, I have kissed. women who were lonely, women I didn't know and didn't want to, but kissed because that was a way to say yes we are still alive and loveable, though separate, women who recognized a loneliness in me, women who were hurt, I confess to kissing the top a 55 year old woman's head in the snow in boston, who was hurt more deeply than I have ever been hurt, and I wanted her as a very few people have wanted me—I wanted her and me to own and control and run the city we lived in, to staff the hospital I knew would mistreat her, to drive the transportation system that had betrayed her, to patrol the streets controlling the men who would murder or disfigure or disrupt us, not accidently with machines, but on purpose, because we are not allowed out on the street alone—

Have you ever committed any indecent acts with women?

Yes, many. I am guilty of allowing suicidal women to die before my eyes or in my ears or under my hands because I thought I could do nothing, I am guilty of leaving a prostitute who held a knife to my friend's throat to keep us from leaving, because we would not sleep with her, we thought

she was old and fat and ugly; I am guilty of not loving her
who needed me; I regret all the women I have not slept with
or comforted, who pulled themselves away from me for lack
of something I had not the courage to fight for, for us, our
life, our planet, our city, our meat and potatoes, our love.
These are indecent acts, lacking courage, lacking a certain
fire behind the eyes, which is the symbol, the raised fist, the
sharing of resources, the resistance that tells death he will
starve for lack of the fat of us, our extra. Yes I have com-
mitted acts of indency with women and most of them were
acts of ommission. I regret them bitterly.

Five
Bless this day oh cat our house

"I was allowed to go
3 places, growing up," she said—
"3 places, no more.
there was a straight line from my house
to school, a straight line from my house
to church, a straight line from my house
to the corner store."
her parents thought something might happen to her.
but nothing ever did.

my lovers teeth are white geese flying above me
my lovers muscles are rope ladders under my hands
we are the river of life and the fat of the land
death, do you tell me I cannot touch this woman?
if we use each other up
on each other
that's a little bit less for you
a little bit less for you, ho

death, ho ho death.

Bless this day oh cat our house
help me be not such a mouse
death tells the woman to stay home
and then breaks in the window.

I read this somewhere, I wasnt there:
In feudal Europe, if a woman committed adultery
her husband would sometimes tie her
down, catch a mouse and trap it
under a cup on her bare belly, until
it gnawed itself out, now are you
afraid of mice?

Six
Dressed as I am, a young man once called
me names in Spanish

a woman who talks to death
is a dirty traitor

inside a hamburger joint and
dressed as I am, a young man once called me
names in Spanish
then he called me queer and slugged me.
first I thought the ceiling had fallen down
but there was the counterman making a ham
sandwich, and there was I spread out on his
counter.

For God's sake I said when

I could talk, this guy is beating me up
can't you call the police or something,
can't you stop him? he looked up from
working on his sandwich, which was *my*
sandwich, I had ordered it. He liked
the way I looked. "There's a pay phone
right across the street" he said.

I couldn't listen to the Spanish language
for weeks afterward, without feeling the
most murderous of urges, the simple
association of one thing to another,
so damned simple.

The next day I went to the police station
to become an outraged citizen
Six big policemen stood in the hall,
all white and dressed as they do
they were well pleased with my story, pleased
at what had gotten beat out of me, so
I left them laughing, went home fast
and locked my door.
For several nights I fantasized the scene
again, this time grabbing a chair
and smashing it over the bastard's head,
killing him. I called him a spic, and
killed him. My face healed. his didnt
no child *in* me.

now when I remember I think:
maybe *he* was Josie's baby.
all the chickens come home to roost,
all of them.

Seven
Death and disfiguration

One Christmas eve my lovers and I
we left the bar, driving home slow
there was a woman lying in the snow
by the side of the road. She was wearing
a bathrobe and no shoes, where were
her shoes? she had turned the snow
pink, under her feet. she was an Asian
woman, didnt speak much English, but
she said a taxi driver beat her up
and raped her, throwing her out of his
care.
what on earth was she doing there
on a street she helped to pay for
but doesn't own?
doesn't she know to stay home?

I am a pervert, therefore I've learned
to keep my hands to myself in public
but I was so drunk that night,
I actually did something loving
I took her in my arms, this woman,
until she could breathe right, and
my friends who are perverts too
they touched her too
we all touched her.
"You're going to be all right"
we lied. She started to cry
"I'm 55 years old" she said
and that said everything.

Six big policemen answered the call
no child *in* them.
they seemed afraid to touch her,
then grabbed her like a corpse and heaved her
on their metal stretcher into the van,
crashing and clumsy.
She was more frightened than before.
they were cold and bored.
'don't leave me' she said.
'she'll be all right' they said.
we left, as we have left all of our lovers
as all lovers leave all lovers
much too soon to get the real loving done.

Eight
a mock interrogation

Why did you get into the cab with him, dressed as you are?

I wanted to go somewhere.

Did you know what the cab driver might do
if you got into the cab with him?

I just wanted to go somewhere.

How many times did you
get into the cab with him?

I dont remember.

If you dont remember, how do you know it happened to
you?

Nine
Hey you death

ho and ho poor death
our lovers teeth are white geese flying above us
our lovers muscles are rope ladders under our hands
even though no women yet go down to the sea in ships
except in their dreams.

only the arrogant invent a quick and meaningful end
for themselves, of their own choosing.
everyone else knows how very slow it happens
how the woman's existence bleeds out her years,
how the child shoots up at ten and is arrested and old
how the man carries a murderous shell within him
and passes it on.

we are the fat of the land, and
we all have our list of casualties

to my lovers I bequeath
the rest of my life

I want nothing left of me for you, ho death
except some fertilizer
for the next batch of us
who do not hold hands with you
who do not embrace you
who try not to work for you
or sacrifice themselves or trust
or believe you, ho ignorant
death, how do you know
we happened to you?

wherever our meat hangs on our own bones
for our own use
your pot is so empty
death, ho death
you shall be poor

CONFRONTATIONS
WITH THE DEVIL
IN THE FORM OF LOVE

1977 ~

This is an unfinished set of poems, inspired after seeing an incredible stage production of Ntozake Shange's poetry: *For Colored Girls Who Have Considered Suicide When The Rainbow Is Enuf.*

I have since learned from reading her introduction to her published book, that she modelled her intricate, sweeping expression of seven Black Ladies' Lives from the Common Woman poems. My goodness. How I love these vital threads passed around among women, especially those of us who are expected to be completely split from each other by class, education, race, age, homophobia. How important this is, to our lives and our literature.

Love, in these poems, is a character, a person. She is not yet developed, and neither is her idea of revolution. I am anxious to see where she will lead me; how it is that she is making connections between everyday life and the powers in the universe. I have wanted to be accurate, provocative, full of intellect rather than dazzled or dreamy-eyed, on the subject of love.

The graphics throughout this book are by two women whose primary concern has also been in reshaping the images we have of women, what our strengths are, when seen through our own eyes. Both Karen Sjöholm and Wendy Cadden take material from natural forms to enhance the force of the women they draw. Karen used a regular lead pencil to make the fascinating figures on page 111. Wendy uses felt tip pens and heavy lines to create faces which are both very familiar and everyday, and at the same time like stone sculptures from a land modern women perceive only in dreams of genuine self-esteem. I hope we can make a use of these images, of all our ideas as we generate them, and act on them.

What do I have if not my 2 hands
& my apples
Look at my lips
they are apples
my eyes are apples
my life is an
apple tree

Love came along   and saved me saved me
Love came along and
after that I did not feel like fighting for
anything anymore after all
didnt I have   not that I had
anything to speak of
OR keep quiet about
but didnt I have
company in my nothing?
someone to say You're Great, to shout you are
wonderful, to whisper to me you are my every little thing?
& then one day Love left to go save someone else.
Love ran off with all my self-esteem my sense of being
wonderful and all my nothing.
now I am in the hole.

you are what is female
you shall be called Eve.
and what is masculine shall be called God.

And from your name Eve we shall take
the word Evil.
and from God's, the word Good.
now you understand patriarchal morality.

Love is a space which is attracted
to energy and repelled by
vacuums.
does that say anything to you
about what irritates me
when you speak only of what you have to need
and never what you need to have to offer?

Jason, hero
everytime we created something
you put on our clothes
and called it yours
           you sat down on our birthing chairs
           & crowned yourself
           the king of life

took the contents of our medicine bags
and appointed yourself
surgeon general
           gathered up our potatoes sheep & yams
           moved into the Dept of Agriculture
           and told us to go on a diet

Jason, trousers were invented
by Queen Semiramis.
when you put them on you called yourself
manly, which meant that you
would pay us the littlest possible amount

to make them for you
you call this: screwing people
Queen Semiramis would have your head for that

Jason you are no good
and you have such a pretty name, too
I wonder who gave it to you.
We should take all your names away from you
and give you one: Mr. Grand Larceny
sentenced to stand aside while we take
all our stuff back where it came from.

Love came along and saved me
saved me   saved
me.
However, my life remains the same as before.
O What shall I do now that I have
what I've always been looking for.

Venus, ever since they knocked
your block off
your face is so vacant
waiting to be moved in on
by men's imaginations.
how could anybody love you?
having the ugliest mug in the world,
the one that's missing.

Love, you wicked dog
so handsome to look at,
so awkward close up
& so unfaithful to good sense.
Whoever feeds you attention
gets you, like it or not. And
all your bad habits come with
you like a pack of fleas.
Wherever I turn for peace of mind
there is the Love dog scratching
at the door of my lonesomeness,
beating her tail against the leg
of my heart
& panting all night with red breath
in my dreams.
Love dog! Get in or out
of the house of my life, stop chewing
on my belongings, the papers &
shoes of my independence.

Look at my hands
they are apples
my breasts
are apples
my heart
is an apple tree

I love her clothes
she made them herself
I love her garden
she grew it herself
I love her children
she raised them herself
I love her house
she built it herself
I love her ideas
she thought them herself
what I hate is her
individualism

Love came along and saved
no one
Love came along, went broke
got busted, was run out of
town and desperately needs—
something. Dont tell her it's Love.

Venus, dear, where are your arms?
if only you were a tree.
they have so many,
& no one thinks less of them for it.

Ah, Love, you smell of petroleum
and overwork
with grease on your fingernails,
paint in your hair
there is a pained look in your eye
from no appreciation
you speak to me of the lilacs
and appleblossoms we ought to have
the banquets we should be serving,
afterwards rubbing each other for hours
with tenderness and genuine
olive oil
someday. Meantime here is your cracked plate
with spaghetti. Wash your hands &
touch me, praise
my cooking. I shall praise your calluses.
we shall dance in the kitchen
of our imagination.

Love rode 1500 miles on a grey
hound bus & climbed in my window
one night to surprise
both of us.
the pleasure of that sleepy
shock has lasted a decade
now or more because she is
always still doing it and I am
always still pleased. I do indeed like
aggressive women
who come half a continent
just for me; I am not saying that patience
is virtuous, Love
like anybody else, comes to those who
wait actively
and leave their windows open.

This is what is so odd
about your death:
that you will be 34 years old
the rest of my life.
We always said that we would be around
we two,
in our old age
& I still believe that,
however when I am 80
you will still be 34,
& how can we ever understand
what each other has been through?

The poverty of Love is when
the people are feeling hopeless
& their anger comes to live
like a bore worm in the apple of their eye

Jason as the surgeon
Jason to me your well—trained hands
are dog's teeth gnashing
near my vital organs.
your prescriptive doctor eyes
are ignorant pits
for me to fall into.

before you pick up that knife
to stick in my life,
here are some orders for you:
leave my breast on my chest
where you found it,
& my ass on the chair where it sits;
leave my brain in the strain
that describes it
& my heart in its own pocket of tears;
leave my my guts in their coil of a serpent,
& my womb in condition to bear.

& anytime unnecessary knifing tempts you
put your razor fingers in your own
mouth, Jason.
bite down hard.

Young Love

Love's grandmother was a relatively
young woman, though completely blind
from diabetes. When Love was nine
she often took her to the doctor.
They lived alone together on Love's
petty thievery & whatever monthly
checks she rescued from the naked
mailbox. Love was already a fox
& her grandmother's sole support,
who had recently lost 4 toes to
gangrene, which would later take her foot
& then her leg. On this particular, eternal
day, the doctor went behind his screen
to write on a prescription pad
in careful, cryptic, doctor script,
a diet   anyone who was not him
could not afford. He was a real breadwinner.
He gave this list to Love, for her to put into accord.
& then he went to dinner.
Love never did decipher
his prescribed solution to their lives,
although she kept the piece of paper
in her one dress pocket
til it faded away
& worked to understand it every day.

Long after her grandmother had died
that summer, Love, until she grew up
& found out better,
believed that if only she had been able
to read the doctor's secret, scribbled letters,
her grandmother would have survived.
——& it was then she began to think
of revolution

I only have one reason for living
and that's you
And if I didn't have you as a
reason for living,
I would think of something else.

after the boss took over
Love had millions of babies
she didnt want—
and loved them anyway,
as the earth loves
even the fruits forced out of her
though she never forgives them

Love said:
look at my years
they are apples
my weeks are apples
my day
is an apple tree

My name is Judith, meaning
She Who Is Praised
I do not want to be called praised
I want to be called The Power of Love.

if Love means protect then whenever I do not
defend you
I cannot call my name Love.
if Love means rebirth then when I see us
dead on our feet
I cannot call my name Love.
if Love means provide & I cannot
provide for you
why would you call my name Love?

do not mistake my breasts
for mounds of potatoes
or my belly for a great roast duck.
do not take my lips for a streak of luck
nor my neck for an appletree,
do not believe my eyes are a warm swarm of bees;
do not get Love mixed up with me.

Don't misunderstand my hands
for a church with a steeple,
open the fingers & out come the people;
nor take my feet to be acres of solid brown earth,
or anything else of infinite worth
to you, my brawny turtledove;
do not get me mixed up with Love.

not until we have ground we call our own
to stand on
& weapons of our own in hand
& some kind of friends around us
will anyone ever call our name Love,
& then when we do we will all call ourselves
grand, muscley names:
the Protection of Love,
the Provision of Love & the
Power of Love.
until then, my sweethearts,
let us speak simply of
romance, which is so much
easier and so much less
than any of us deserve.